THRIVING

ON

A SHOESTRING

BUDGET

A Guide to Nourishing Your Family of Four

with $300 for a Month

By: Corwin Watson And Janine Madison

Thriving on a Shoestring Budget: A Guide to Nourishing Your Family on $300 to $400 a Month

Published by Rebuild US Publishing

For permission requests, contact the publisher at:

Rebuild US Publishing

www.rebuildnus.com

rebuildnus@gmail.com

ISBN:

First Edition: September 1, 2024

978-1-7378436-1-0

Also, By

Corwin Watson and Janine Madison

The THRIVING ON A SHOESTRING BUDGET SERIES:

Thriving on A Shoestring Budget: A Guide to Nourishing Your Family of Four As A Vegan with $300 for a Month

Also, By

Corwin Watson

Road to Nowhere: How I'm Saving Myself from the Self-Destructive Behaviors that Rules Me-Memoir

From Anger to Peace: A Journey of Love and Healing

A Letter to My Mother

I Know You Want to Get Over: Understanding the Connection Between Driving Behavior and Character

Becoming My Father

SIGN UP FOR MY AUTHOR NEWSLETTER

Be the first to learn about Corwin Watson's new releases and receive exclusive content for readers and writers!

www.rebuildnus.com

DEDICATION

To all the families striving to build a better future. This book is dedicated to you—may you find the strength, knowledge, and determination to thrive, no matter the challenges.

ACKNOWLEDGMENTS

This book would not have been possible without the support of our families, friends, and the many individuals who have shared their experiences and insights along the way. We are grateful for the opportunity to share our knowledge and help others thrive on a budget.

Table of Contents

INTRODUCTION

Welcome to "Thriving on a Shoestring Budget: A Guide to Nourishing Your Family on $300 to $400 a Month." In these pages, you'll discover practical strategies, creative recipes, and savvy tips to not just survive but thrive by managing your family's needs on a tight budget. From meal planning to smart shopping, let's embark on a journey to delicious, nutritious, and budget-friendly eating.

Chapter 1

BREAKING THE CYCLE: OVERCOMING FINANCIAL CHALLENGES

YOU MIGHT BE WONDERING how a seemingly arbitrary number like $300 a month or $75 a week for groceries became my reality. It may sound like I'm feeding a family straight out of a comic book, where everyone has the appetite of a small bird. But let me assure you, my family is anything but small in size or appetite. Our household is in a perpetual state of growth, with children who seem to be constantly hungry. The ongoing joke at home is the never-ending chorus of

"Can I have a snack?"—a question that even pops up in the middle of dinner, a testament to the bottomless pit that is a growing child's stomach. Even now, as I sit to write this, my five-year-old has interrupted multiple times, rubbing her belly and reminding me that it's time for another snack.

Facing Financial Realities

So, when faced with the challenge of feeding this ever-hungry crew on a tight budget, I completely understand why it might seem impossible at first glance. But here's the surprising truth: through careful planning, resourcefulness, and a fair amount of culinary creativity, we found out that it is not only possible but entirely doable to stretch those dollars without sacrificing taste or nutrition. And that's what this chapter—and this entire book—is about: inspiring you to take control of your finances, not just to survive, but to thrive, and to lead your family towards better financial health and well-being.

The Impact of Financial Challenges

When my family was unexpectedly reduced to a budget of $75 a week, the impact was immediate and profound. It sparked indignation in my then-wife, who felt frustrated and overwhelmed by the constraints. I won't lie—my own ego and pride took a significant hit. There's a particular kind of pain that comes from knowing you can't provide abundantly for your loved ones, and that feeling can be paralyzing. But here's something I've learned: where you are financially is often the result of an accumulation of decisions over time. Sure, social economics and the environment you grow up in play significant roles in shaping your opportunities, but we all have to face the reality that our choices, influenced by our experiences and traumas, have brought us to where we are today.

The Need for Change

During my military career, I faced various transitions—from the rigid structure of service life to the often chaotic and unpredictable world of civilian life. Despite my training, resilience, and expertise in handling high-stress situations, managing money remained a persistent struggle. Looking back, it's clear that coming from an environment steeped in trauma influenced my financial decisions. Impulse spending became my default mode, a way to cope with underlying stress and unresolved emotions. But the thing about trauma is that it doesn't just disappear; it manifests in different ways, and for me, it led to financial ruin. My lack of financial literacy was a direct result of my upbringing and the financial woes that plagued my adult life.

A Wake-Up Call

The turning point for me was when I had to confront the harsh reality of my financial mismanagement. It wasn't easy—looking in the mirror and acknowledging my failures was one of the hardest things I've ever had to do. But it was also the first step toward change. I began to understand that my financial troubles weren't just about dollars and cents—they were about the deeper issues of trauma, fear, and survival. And once I recognized that, I could start taking the steps necessary to change my financial trajectory and, by extension, the way my family engages with food and money.

Breaking the Cycle

This wake-up call underscored the importance of breaking the cycle of financial mismanagement. It became clear that identifying the impulse to spend, acknowledging past mistakes, and embracing proactive approaches to financial management were imperative. But breaking these cycles requires more than just practical strategies—it requires empathy and an understanding of the profound impact that trauma can have on our financial decisions. Being introspective is key to identifying the problem, but without the right strategies and tools, self-awareness alone isn't enough. It's about unraveling the complex web of emotions and beliefs that govern our financial choices and finding ways to move forward.

Despite the setbacks and challenges, I'm here to tell you that financial empowerment is achievable. It's not going to happen overnight, and it's not going to be easy, but with diligent discipline and unwavering commitment, you can break the cycle of financial hardships. By embracing the principles of frugality, resourcefulness, and collaboration, it's possible to not only survive on a tight budget but to thrive and build a brighter future for yourself and your loved ones.

Chapter 2

UNDERSTANDING YOUR BUDGET AND SETTING UP A VISION BOARD FOR LONG-TERM SUCCESS

Introduction

The first step on the path to thriving on a shoestring budget is gaining a deep understanding of your financial situation. It's not just about knowing how much money you have; it's about understanding where every dollar goes and how to make each one work for you. This chapter will guide you through breaking down your expenses, identifying areas where you can save money, and laying the groundwork for successful budgeting.

Budgeting Basics

To start, sit down with your partner or family members and have an honest discussion about your household income and expenses. Include food as a dedicated budget item, allocating $300 for the month. In the beginning, you might need to spend closer to $400 to stock up on essentials that will help reduce costs later. Together, compile a list of all the products you'll need for meal planning, including those recommended in this book. This initial investment will set you up for success as you learn to stretch your dollars further each month.

Discipline and Financial Planning

Understanding your budget isn't just about crunching numbers—it's about making informed decisions and sticking tightly to your financial plan. In the first few months, it's essential to adhere to your budget as closely as possible to avoid the discomfort of adjustment. This discipline will not only help you navigate the initial challenges but also empower you to plan meals, prep in advance, and set the stage for long-term success.

Creating a Vision Board

One powerful way to jumpstart this process is by creating a vision board. A vision board isn't just a fun project; it's a powerful tool for staying focused and motivated on your financial journey. Here's how to create a vision board tailored to your financial goals:

Define Your Goals: Start by clearly defining your financial and personal goals. This could range from sticking to your food budget, preparing healthier meals, or even long-term objectives like buying a home. Specifically, set goals for what food you're going to prepare, how you're going to budget for it, and the savings you hope to achieve. This will help you reverse the financial and physical damage caused by poor eating habits and financial mismanagement.

Gather Materials: Collect materials for your vision board, such as magazines, newspapers, images, quotes, and other visuals that resonate with your goals. This step can be a fun family activity—get your kids involved so they understand the stakes and the rewards of financial discipline.

Select Images and Quotes: Choose visuals that evoke a sense of determination, focus, and achievement. These could include pictures of healthy meals, savings milestones, or quotes about discipline and financial freedom. You might also include images from your favorite cooking shows or articles that inspire you to prepare and preserve food creatively.

Arrange and Design: Arrange your selected images and quotes on the board or canvas in a way that is visually appealing and motivating. You can organize them thematically or create a timeline of your goals, showing the progress from where you are now to where you want to be.

Visualize Your Success: Use the vision board to help you visualize success. Imagine your fridge stocked with healthy, budget-friendly foods that energize your family. Extend this visualization to other goals, like seeing your savings account grow or finally paying off that lingering debt.

Review Regularly: Set aside time each week to review your vision board with your family. This is a great way to reflect on your progress, reassess your goals if necessary, and stay committed to your journey. It's also an opportunity to involve your children in discussions about money, helping them develop healthy financial habits early on.

Take Action: Remember that a vision board is more than just a collage—it's a tool to inspire action. Use it as a daily reminder of why you're striving for financial discipline and take consistent steps toward your goals.

Creating a vision board is a fun and effective way to bring your financial goals to life. It provides a visual representation of your aspirations and serves as a daily reminder to stay focused and motivated. To make it even more effective, categorize your goals into sections like "things you want to accomplish," "things you have started," and "things completed." As goals move from left to right, you'll get a clear picture of your progress, which can be incredibly motivating.

Establishing a Routine

In addition to creating a vision board, establishing a routine is crucial. Setting up a daily or weekly routine can help instill discipline and consistency in your budgeting practices. Designate specific times for meal planning, grocery shopping, and meal prep, making these tasks non-negotiable parts of your schedule. Keep track of every dollar spent by using budgeting tools or apps, which can help you monitor your spending habits and identify areas where you can cut back or adjust.

Practicing Self-Control

Practicing self-control is another key component of successful budgeting. Before making a purchase, ask yourself if it aligns with your financial goals and whether it's truly necessary.

Avoid shopping when you're hungry, and always distinguish between wants and needs.

Finally, celebrate your progress. Acknowledge small victories along the way to reinforce positive habits. Whether it's reaching a savings milestone or sticking to your meal plan for the week, these achievements will motivate you to continue moving forward.

BUDGET

Chapter 3

MEAL PLANNING 101 – MAXIMIZING SAVINGS AND FLAVOR

Introduction

Meal planning is much more than just deciding what to eat each day; it's a strategic approach to stretching your dollar while savoring delicious, nutritious meals that nourish your family. This chapter will guide you through the art of planning meals around sales, seasonal produce, and pantry staples, empowering you to maximize your budget without compromising on taste or nutrition. It's also about making intentional choices that build stronger family bonds, improve your health, and save you money in the long run.

Planning Around Sales

One of the most effective strategies for cost-effective meal planning is keeping an eye on sales at your local grocery store. Sales can provide opportunities to stock up on essentials at a fraction of the cost, helping you make the most of your budget. Here's how to maximize savings by planning around sales:

Subscribe to Newsletters: Many grocery stores offer newsletters that include weekly deals and promotions. Sign up for these to stay informed about upcoming sales, so you can plan your meals accordingly.

Check Weekly Flyers: Most grocery stores release weekly flyers with their current sales. Make it a habit to review these before planning your meals. Planning your meals around what's on sale can significantly reduce your grocery bill.

Use Mobile Apps: Apps like Flipp and Grocery Pal aggregate sales and discounts from multiple stores, making it easier to compare prices and plan your shopping trips effectively.

Stock Up on Essentials: When you find a great deal on pantry staples or items you frequently use, consider buying in bulk. Just be mindful of expiration dates to avoid waste, and think about how you can incorporate these items into your meals over time.

Embracing Seasonal Produce

Seasonal produce not only enhances the flavor and nutrition of your meals but also helps you save money. Fruits and vegetables that are in season are often more abundant, fresher, and cheaper than their out-of-season counterparts. Here's how to make the most of seasonal produce:

Explore Farmers' Markets: Farmers' markets are excellent sources of fresh, seasonal produce. Shopping here supports local farmers and often provides better deals on fruits and vegetables. Plus, the produce is usually fresher and more flavorful.

Join CSA Programs: Community Supported Agriculture (CSA) programs allow you to buy shares of a local farm's harvest. These programs can provide a variety of fresh produce at a lower cost, and it's a great way to introduce your family to new fruits and vegetables.

Ask About Seasonality: Inquire at your local grocery store about what's in season. Many stores highlight seasonal produce, making it easier to identify and purchase these items at their peak quality and price.

Plan Around Seasonal Ingredients: Base your meals around what's in season to enjoy variety, freshness, and affordability.

Seasonal ingredients can inspire new recipes and add excitement to your meals, turning meal planning into a fun and creative process.

Harnessing Pantry Staples

Pantry staples are the backbone of budget-friendly meal planning. These shelf-stable ingredients, such as grains, legumes, canned goods, and spices, form the foundation of countless recipes and are essential for stretching your budget. Here's how to effectively harness pantry staples:

Regular Inventory Checks: Take inventory of your pantry regularly to know what you have and avoid unnecessary purchases. This practice helps you plan meals around what's already available, reducing waste and saving money. It's a simple yet powerful strategy to stay organized and make the most of your resources.

Replenish Essentials: Maintain a well-stocked pantry by replenishing essentials as needed. Items like rice, pasta, beans, and canned tomatoes are versatile and can be used in a variety of dishes. Keeping these staples on hand ensures that you're always prepared to whip up a meal, even on short notice.

Get Creative with Recipes: Experiment with recipes that use pantry staples as their base. Soups, stews, casseroles, and stir-fries are great ways to use these ingredients creatively, and they can be easily adapted to include seasonal produce or leftovers.

Minimize Perishables: While fresh produce is important, relying too heavily on perishable items can lead to waste. Balance your meal plan with a mix of fresh and pantry-staple ingredients to ensure you're using what you have before it goes bad.

The Importance of Maximizing Family Savings and Flavor

Meal planning is not just a practical tool for saving money; it's an opportunity to enhance your family's well-being by fostering healthier eating habits and stronger relationships. When you plan meals carefully, you're not just feeding your family—you're investing in their health, happiness, and future.

Contrast with Eating Out

In contrast, eating out, especially at fast food restaurants, often seems convenient but comes with hidden costs. For example, a meal for a family of four at a fast-food chain like Chick-fil-A or Burger King can easily cost $30 to $40. While this might seem like a reasonable price for the convenience, consider what that same $30 to $40 could buy at the grocery store. With careful planning, you could purchase ingredients to prepare multiple meals, providing your family with healthy, home-cooked food for several days.

Not only does eating out strain your budget, but it also limits your ability to control the nutritional content of your meals. Fast food is often high in unhealthy fats, sugars, and sodium, contributing to long-term health issues such as obesity, heart disease, and diabetes. Processed foods, which are prevalent in fast food and many packaged meals, have been linked to various health problems, including metabolic disorders and chronic inflammation. By contrast, home-cooked meals allow you to choose wholesome, nutritious ingredients that support your family's health.

The Misconception that Eating Healthy is Expensive

A common misconception is that eating healthy is more expensive than eating processed or fast foods. However, this is not necessarily true. When you factor in the long-term costs of poor health, the expense of medical bills, and the reduced quality of life, the cost of unhealthy eating far outweighs the initial savings. In reality, with strategic meal planning, you can prepare healthy, satisfying meals on a budget.

Healthy eating can be affordable when you focus on whole foods like grains, legumes, and seasonal produce, which are often less expensive than processed foods. By buying in bulk, shopping sales, and planning meals around affordable, nutrient-dense foods, you can eat well without breaking the bank.

HARNESSING
PANTRY
STAPLES

Chapter 4

SMART SHOPPING TECHNIQUES – STRETCHING YOUR BUDGET LIKE A PRO

Introduction

Shopping smart is crucial when you're trying to stretch a small budget. It's about making every dollar count and avoiding the traps that lead to unnecessary spending. In this chapter, you'll learn techniques like buying in bulk, comparison shopping, and taking advantage of coupons and loyalty programs. These skills will enable you to maximize your savings without sacrificing quality, helping you thrive on a shoestring budget. We'll also explore how immediate gratification and poor financial discipline can lead to failure, while smart shopping can set you up for long-term success.

Buying in Bulk

Buying in bulk is a savvy way to slice your grocery bill. Stocking up on items like rice, beans, pasta, and other non-perishables in larger quantities often comes with significant cost savings per unit. However, it's essential to approach bulk buying with a plan to avoid waste and ensure you're actually saving money. Here are some tips for buying in bulk effectively:

Assess Your Storage Space: Before purchasing bulk items, ensure you have enough storage space. Invest in airtight containers to keep food fresh and prevent pests. Lack of storage is one of the biggest pitfalls when buying in bulk—if food spoils or goes bad, you're losing money rather than saving it.

Prioritize Non-Perishables: Focus on buying non-perishable items in bulk, such as grains, canned goods, and spices. These items have long shelf lives and can be used in a variety of meals. They're the backbone of budget-friendly meal planning.

Shop at Bulk Retailers: Stores like Costco, Sam's Club, and local co-ops offer bulk buying options. Compare membership costs and benefits to determine the best option for your family. Sometimes, buying in bulk requires an upfront investment, but the long-term savings can be substantial.

Buy What You Use: Avoid the temptation to buy in bulk just because it's cheaper. Stick to items you know your family will use to prevent waste. If you find yourself throwing away expired food, it's a sign that bulk buying may not be the best strategy for that particular item.

Rotate Stock: Use the oldest items first to ensure nothing goes to waste. Regularly check expiration dates and organize your pantry accordingly. This is a key technique that expert shoppers use to avoid the "out of sight, out of mind" problem that leads to wasted food.

Comparison Shopping

Comparison shopping is a powerful tool for finding the best deals. Whether you prefer shopping online or browsing newspaper circulars, comparing prices across multiple retailers can help you save money. Here's how to navigate both online and offline channels:

Use Online Platforms: Websites and apps like Google Shopping, PriceGrabber, and Honey allow you to quickly compare prices across multiple retailers. Take advantage of these tools to find the best deals without leaving your home. This can save you both time and money, especially when shopping for specific, higher-priced items.

Scan Newspaper Ads: Traditional newspaper ads often feature local deals and discounts that might not be advertised online. Regularly review these circulars to spot opportunities for savings. Sometimes, the best deals are found in places you least expect, like your local newspaper.

Check Store Websites: Many stores post their weekly ads and special promotions on their websites. Bookmark your favorite stores and review their deals before planning your shopping trip. This practice is particularly useful during holiday seasons or special sales events.

Create a Price Book: Track the prices of items you frequently buy across different stores. This will help you identify the best places to shop for specific items and recognize genuine deals. Over time, you'll develop a sense of what constitutes a good price, which can protect you from falling for marketing gimmicks.

Be Flexible: Sometimes, shopping at multiple stores can yield better savings than sticking to one retailer. Be open to visiting different stores to take advantage of the best prices. While it might require more effort, the savings can add up significantly over time.

Taking Advantage of Coupons and Loyalty Programs

Coupons and loyalty programs are valuable assets in the arsenal of savvy shoppers. Coupons offer instant savings on specific items or provide discounts on your total purchase. Meanwhile, loyalty programs can reward you for your consistent patronage with points, discounts, or even free items. Here's how to maximize their benefits:

Collect Coupons: Start collecting coupons from newspapers, online coupon sites, and store apps. Organize them by category and expiration date to ensure you use them before they expire. Expert shoppers know that a well-organized coupon collection is key to maximizing savings.

Use Store Loyalty Programs: Sign up for loyalty programs at your favorite stores to earn points, receive exclusive discounts, and get early access to sales. These programs often offer personalized discounts based on your shopping habits, allowing you to save even more.

Combine Coupons and Sales: The best deals often come when you combine coupons with in-store sales. For example, if you have a coupon for 50 cents off a product that's already on sale, you can maximize your savings. This strategy can lead to significant discounts, sometimes even making items free or close to it.

Digital Coupons and Apps: Many stores now offer digital coupons that can be loaded directly onto your loyalty card. Apps like Ibotta and Rakuten also offer cash back for purchases made at participating stores. These tools make it easier than ever to save money without the hassle of clipping physical coupons.

Stay Disciplined: It's easy to get carried away with coupons and loyalty programs, buying items you don't really need just because they're discounted. Stay disciplined and only use coupons for items you would have bought anyway. Remember, the goal is to save money, not to stockpile things you won't use.

The Pitfalls of Poor Shopping Techniques

Smart shopping isn't just about knowing what to do—it's also about understanding what not to do. Poor shopping techniques can lead to wasted money, food, and opportunities. Here's an anecdotal story to illustrate this point:

I once met a family who struggled financially yet found themselves eating out frequently, especially at fast-food chains. They were drawn in by the immediate gratification and convenience, often spending $30 to $40 per meal at places like Burger King or Chick-fil-A. What they didn't realize was that this spending added up quickly—often exceeding $1,000 a month on fast food alone. When I compared this to the cost of buying groceries, it became clear that the same $30 to $40 could easily cover several days' worth of nutritious, home-cooked meals. Not only would they have saved money, but they also would have provided their children with healthier food and more opportunities to bond as a family.

This family's story is a cautionary tale about the dangers of immediate gratification and poor financial discipline. When we choose fast food over home-cooked meals, we're not just spending more money—we're also sacrificing our health and missing out on the opportunity to teach our children valuable life skills.

The Marketing Ploys of Grocery Chains

Grocery chains are masters at getting you to spend more than you intended. From strategically placing high-margin items at eye level to offering "buy one, get one free" deals that tempt you to buy more than you need, these tactics are designed to separate you from your money. Here's how to outsmart them:

Stick to Your List: Before you go shopping, make a list of what you need and stick to it. This will help you avoid impulse purchases that can quickly add up.

Shop the Perimeter: Grocery stores often place the most nutritious, whole foods—like produce, meat, and dairy—around the perimeter of the store. By shopping the perimeter first, you can fill your cart with healthy essentials before venturing into the more tempting aisles.

Beware of Endcaps: The displays at the ends of aisles, known as endcaps, are often used to promote high-margin items or those that are on sale. While these deals might seem enticing, they're not always the best value. Compare prices with similar items in the main aisles to ensure you're getting the best deal.

Understand Unit Pricing: Many stores display the unit price of items on the shelf label. This tells you how much you're paying per ounce, pound, or other unit of measure. Use this information to compare the cost of different brands or package sizes.

Teaching Children Smart Shopping Techniques

Teaching your children smart shopping techniques is an investment in their future. It equips them with the skills they need to make informed decisions, avoid marketing traps, and manage their own finances effectively. Here's how to get started:

Involve Them in the Process: Take your children shopping with you and explain the strategies you're using to save money. Show them how to compare prices, use coupons, and choose nutritious foods.

Set a Budget: Give your children a small budget and let them help plan a meal or pick out a snack. This teaches them the value of money and how to make choices within a budget.

Discuss Marketing Tricks: Talk to your children about how stores use marketing tricks to get people to spend more. Teach them to be skeptical of flashy packaging and "too good to be true" deals.

Learn About Food Bans: Educate your children about the fact that many of the processed foods we eat in the United States are banned in other countries due to health concerns. Discuss why it's important to choose whole, unprocessed foods whenever possible.

Growing Your Own Food

One of the most effective ways to save money and ensure your family is eating healthy, unprocessed food is to grow your own. Whether you have a large garden or just a few pots on the balcony, growing your own produce can reduce your grocery bill and provide a valuable learning experience for your children.

Start Small: If you're new to gardening, start with a few easy-to-grow plants like tomatoes, lettuce, or herbs. These can be grown in small spaces and provide fresh produce throughout the growing season.

Involve the Family: Gardening is a great way to spend time together as a family. Involve your children in planting, watering, and harvesting. This teaches them where food comes from and gives them a sense of accomplishment.

Preserve the Harvest: Learn how to can, freeze, or dry your homegrown produce so you can enjoy it year-round. This not only saves money but also ensures you have healthy, homegrown food even in the off-season.

Reduce Waste: Compost kitchen scraps and garden waste to create nutrient-rich soil for your garden. This reduces waste and improves the quality of your garden.

Breaking the Cycle of Immediate Gratification

Finally, it's important to recognize that shopping smart is about more than just saving money. It's about breaking the cycle of immediate gratification that leads so many families into financial trouble. When we prioritize convenience and impulse purchases over planning and discipline, we set ourselves up for failure.

Instead, we need to embrace the long-term benefits of smart shopping. By planning our meals, sticking to a budget, and making intentional choices, we can improve our financial situation, our health, and our relationships. This isn't just about learning to shop smarter—it's about learning to live smarter.

Chapter 5

REDUCING WASTE – MAKING THE MOST OF WHAT YOU HAVE

Introduction

The old adage "waste not, want not" couldn't be more true when you're living on a tight budget, especially in a world where food prices are constantly on the rise. Making the most of what you have and avoiding the waste of perfectly good food is crucial not just for your wallet but for the environment as well. In this chapter, we'll explore strategies for reducing food waste, making the most of leftovers, and repurposing ingredients to stretch your budget. We'll also discuss the broader implications of food waste in the United States and the importance of changing our mindset.

The Cost of Food Waste

According to the Food and Agricultural Organization of the United Nations, around one-third of all food produced for human consumption is lost or wasted. This statistic is alarming, not only because of the waste of money but also due to the precious resources such as water, energy, and labor that are squandered in the process. In the United States alone, billions of pounds of food are wasted each year, contributing to environmental degradation and economic inefficiency. Reducing food waste in your own home can have a significant impact on both your budget and the environment.

Planning and Shopping Smart

Reducing food waste starts long before the food even reaches your kitchen. It begins with thoughtful planning and smart shopping. Here's how to get started:

Meal Planning

Start by planning your meals ahead of time and only buying what you need. A well-thought-out meal plan can help you avoid impulse purchases and ensure you use up all the food you buy.

Create a Weekly Menu: Outline what your family will eat for breakfast, lunch, and dinner each day of the week. Don't forget to include snacks and desserts if needed.

Make a Grocery List: Based on your meal plan, write a detailed grocery list. Stick to this list to avoid buying unnecessary items.

Check Your Pantry: Before heading to the store, check your pantry, fridge, and freezer to see what you already have. This will help you avoid buying duplicates and use up items you already have.

Smart Shopping

When you go shopping, it's crucial to make thoughtful choices to prevent waste:

Buy in Bulk (When It Makes Sense): Bulk buying can save money, but only if you can use or properly store the items. Non-perishable items like rice, pasta, and canned goods are ideal for bulk purchases.

Choose Seasonal Produce: Seasonal fruits and vegetables are often fresher and cheaper. They also tend to have a longer shelf life, which helps reduce waste.

Avoid Impulse Buys: Stick to your grocery list. Impulse buys often lead to unnecessary expenses and potential food waste.

Shop with Sales in Mind: Take advantage of sales and discounts, but only for items you know you will use before they expire.

Proper Food Storage

Once you've done your shopping, the next step in reducing waste is proper food storage. Storing your food correctly can extend its shelf life and prevent spoilage.

Fruits and Vegetables

Use the Crisper Drawer: Store fruits and vegetables in the crisper drawer of your fridge to keep them fresh longer. Different types of produce have different storage needs; for instance, leafy greens should be stored in a separate drawer from fruits to prevent ethylene gas from causing them to spoil faster.

Paper Towels: Place a paper towel in the bottom of your storage containers to absorb excess moisture, which can cause fruits and vegetables to rot more quickly.

Freeze Excess Produce: If you have more fresh produce than you can use, consider freezing it. Most fruits and vegetables freeze well and can be used later in smoothies, soups, or stews.

Meat and Dairy

Store Meat in the Coldest Part of the Fridge: The bottom shelf is typically the coldest part of the fridge and is ideal for storing meat.

Use Original Containers: Keep dairy products in their original containers to maintain their freshness. Make sure to seal them properly after each use.

Pantry Staples

Airtight Containers: Store dry goods like flour, sugar, and pasta in airtight containers to keep them fresh and prevent pests.

Label and Rotate: Label containers with the purchase date and use older items first. This method, known as "first in, first out," helps reduce waste.

Portion Control and Leftovers

Smart Portioning

One of the primary sources of food waste is cooking or serving more food than your family can consume. Here are some tips to help with portion control:

Know Serving Sizes: Familiarize yourself with standard serving sizes for different foods. This can help you prepare the right amount for each meal.

Smaller Plates for Kids: Children often have smaller appetites, so using smaller plates can help ensure they aren't served more than they can eat.

Encourage Mindful Eating: Teach your children to eat slowly and listen to their hunger cues. This can help prevent overeating and reduce waste.

Making the Most of Leftovers

Leftovers are a great way to save time and money, but they can also become a source of food waste if not used promptly. Here are some ideas to make the most of leftovers:

Plan for Leftovers: When planning your meals, consider how you can repurpose leftovers. For example, if you roast a chicken for dinner, plan to use the leftover meat in sandwiches or salads the next day.

Proper Storage: Store leftovers in airtight containers and label them with the date. Use clear containers so you can easily see what's inside.

Repurpose Ingredients: Get creative with leftovers. Turn leftover roasted vegetables into a frittata, use cooked grains in a salad, or transform cooked meat into a new dish like tacos or stir-fry.

Creative Repurposing of Ingredients

Repurposing ingredients can stretch your budget and reduce waste. Here are some ideas for making the most of common ingredients:

Chicken

Sandwiches and Salads: Slice leftover chicken breasts for sandwiches or shred the meat for salads.

Toppings: Use shredded chicken as a topping for baked potatoes or pizzas.

Soups and Stews: Add leftover chicken to soups or stews for added protein.

Potatoes

Homemade Chips: Use a potato cutter to slice potatoes thinly, season them, and bake or air-fry for homemade chips.

Baked Potatoes: Make baked potatoes and top them with sour cream, cheese, and chives for a hearty meal.

Sauteed Potatoes: Dice baked potatoes and sauté them with onions for a delicious side dish.

Bread

French Toast: Use stale bread to make French toast.

Croutons: Cut bread into cubes, season, and bake to make croutons for salads.

Bread Crumbs: Process stale bread into bread crumbs for use in meatballs, coatings, or toppings.

Rice

Fried Rice: Use leftover rice to make fried rice with vegetables and a protein.

Rice Pudding: Turn leftover rice into a sweet treat by making rice pudding.

Stuffed Peppers: Mix cooked rice with ground meat and vegetables to stuff bell peppers.

Vegetables

Smoothies: Blend wilting vegetables like spinach or kale into smoothies.

Soups: Chop and freeze leftover vegetables to use in soups or stews.

Stir-Fry: Use leftover vegetables in a quick stir-fry with a protein and sauce.

Dairy

Yogurt: Use yogurt nearing its expiration date in smoothies or as a base for salad dressings.

Milk: Use milk in baking or to make homemade sauces.

Cheese: Grate and freeze cheese to use later in cooking.

The Distractions and Disciplines Around Eating Leftovers

There's no denying that leftovers often get a bad rap. With the convenience of fast food restaurants and services promising quick delivery, it's no wonder that many of us think so lowly of leftovers. The immediate gratification of a fresh meal delivered to your door is hard to compete with, but this mindset contributes to the epidemic of food waste in the United States.

We need to change our perspective on leftovers. Instead of seeing them as less desirable, we should view them as an opportunity to save time, money, and resources. Leftovers can be just as delicious as the original meal, and with a little creativity, they can even be transformed into something new and exciting.

It's also important to recognize the role that discipline plays in reducing food waste. It requires effort and commitment to plan meals, store food properly, and make use of leftovers. But the benefits—both financial and environmental—are well worth the effort.

The Epidemic of Food Waste in the United States

Food waste is a significant problem in the United States, with millions of tons of food being thrown away each year. This waste not only represents a loss of valuable resources but also contributes to environmental issues such as greenhouse gas emissions from decomposing food in landfills.

Changing our mindset is crucial if we want to reverse this epidemic. Guilt alone—whether about the wasted food or the starving children around the world—hasn't proven to be an effective motivator. Instead, we need to focus on the practical benefits of reducing food waste, such as saving money, improving health, and taking care of our planet.

Practical Tips to Reverse the Epidemic of Wasting Food

Grow Your Own Produce: Growing your own fruits and vegetables can help reduce food waste by providing fresh, organic produce that you can harvest as needed. It also saves money and teaches valuable skills that can be passed down through generations.

Composting: Start a compost bin for food scraps that can't be used in cooking. Composting reduces waste and provides nutrient-rich soil for your garden.

Buy Ony One, One,
Geet One Free

Chapter 6

THRIVING ON A SHOESTRING BUDGET

Introduction

Thriving on a shoestring budget may require adjustments, sacrifices, and a shift in mindset, but it is absolutely doable. This final chapter will recap the key points covered in this book and provide additional tips to help you stay on track with your budget. By applying the strategies outlined, you can nourish your family of four with just $300 a month. While it may take time and effort to adjust to this new way of living, the rewards—both financial and personal—are well worth it. Happy budgeting!

Recap of Key Strategies

Meal planning is the cornerstone of a budget-friendly lifestyle. By planning your meals around sales, seasonal produce, and pantry staples, you can maximize your budget without compromising on nutrition or flavor. Here are the key takeaways from our meal planning strategies:

Plan Around Sales: Keep an eye on grocery store flyers, newsletters, and apps to stay informed about sales. Plan your meals around discounted items to stretch your budget further.

Embrace Seasonal Produce: Seasonal fruits and vegetables are fresher, more flavorful, and usually cheaper than out-of-season alternatives. Incorporate them into your meal plans to save money and enjoy a variety of nutritious foods.

Utilize Pantry Staples: Keep your pantry stocked with versatile, non-perishable items like grains, legumes, canned goods, and spices. These staples form the foundation of countless recipes and help you whip up meals even when fresh ingredients are running low.

Smart Shopping Techniques

Smart shopping is essential for stretching your budget. Here are some techniques to help you shop more effectively:

Buy in Bulk: Purchasing items like rice, beans, pasta, and other non-perishables in bulk can save you money in the long run. Just make sure you have adequate storage space and containers to keep these items fresh.

Comparison Shopping: Compare prices across different stores, both online and offline, to find the best deals. Use apps and websites that aggregate prices to make this process easier.

Coupons and Loyalty Programs: Take advantage of coupons and loyalty programs to save money. Collect and organize coupons, and use loyalty programs to earn rewards and access exclusive discounts.

Reducing Waste

Reducing food waste is one of the most effective ways to save money and make the most of your groceries. Here are some tips to help you minimize waste:

Proper Storage: Store food properly to extend its shelf life. Keep fruits and vegetables in the crisper drawer, store meat in the coldest part of the fridge, and use airtight containers for pantry staples.

Smart Portioning: Prepare portion sizes that match your family's needs to avoid overloading plates and wasting food. Teach children to serve themselves smaller portions and go back for seconds if they are still hungry.

Creative Repurposing: Get creative with leftovers and unused ingredients. Turn roasted chicken into sandwiches or salads, use leftover rice for fried rice, and repurpose vegetables in soups or stir-fries.

Overcoming the Scarcity Mentality

One of the most challenging aspects of thriving on a tight budget is overcoming the scarcity mentality—the fear that there won't be enough. This mindset often stems from past experiences of lack or insecurity and can lead to impulsive spending, hoarding, or overconsumption. It's essential to recognize and address these fears, replacing them with a mindset of abundance and resourcefulness.

The Importance of Knowledge

Knowledge is power, especially when it comes to budgeting and meal planning. The more you understand about nutrition, smart shopping, and food storage, the better equipped you are to make decisions that benefit your family's health and financial well-being. Continuous learning—whether through reading, attending workshops, or experimenting in the kitchen—can help you develop the skills needed to thrive on a limited budget.

Turning Off the Distractions

In today's world, we are constantly bombarded by food commercials, advertisements, and marketing ploys designed to tempt us into buying more than we need. These distractions can make it difficult to stick to a budget or maintain healthy eating habits. It's important to recognize the hidden agenda of food manufacturers, who often cooperate with Wall Street, psychologists, and advertisers to keep us distracted, overfed, and unhealthy.

To combat this, practice mindfulness when making food choices. Turn off the TV, unsubscribe from marketing emails, and focus on your family's actual needs rather than succumbing to external pressures. By taking control of your environment, you can make more intentional, informed decisions that align with your budget and health goals.

Sample Weekly Meal Plan

Creating a meal plan for an entire week can help you stay on budget and ensure your family is well-fed. Below is a sample meal plan for a family of four, covering breakfast, lunch, and dinner for a week.

Week One

Breakfast:

Days 1-2: Cream of wheat with cinnamon and a slice of toast

Days 3-4: Two slices of French toast with your choice of meat and maple syrup or homemade flavoring

Days 5-6: Bowl of oatmeal with cinnamon, butter, and brown sugar or your preferred sweetener

Day 7: Scrambled eggs with toast and a side of fruit

Lunch:

Days 1-2: Peanut butter and jelly sandwiches with apple slices

Days 3-4: Chicken salad wraps (using leftover chicken) with carrot sticks

Days 5-6: Bean and cheese quesadillas with salsa and a side of sliced bell peppers

Day 7: Homemade vegetable soup with a side of whole-grain crackers

Dinner:

Days 1-2: Spaghetti with half a pack of large ground beef, spaghetti sauce, onion, and dinner rolls with butter and garlic

Days 3-4: Chili with the second half of the ground beef, onion, beans, and your choice of seasoning, served with water flavored with lemon or mint

Days 5-6: Baked potatoes topped with leftover chili, cheese, onion, sautéed peppers, jalapeños, and any other preferred toppings

Day 7: Mashed potatoes seasoned to your liking, with chicken breast (sliced in half to stretch the portions) either pan-fried, air-fried, or baked, served with a dinner roll

Week Two

Breakfast:

Days 1-2: Greek yogurt with honey and granola

Days 3-4: Smoothie made with frozen fruit, spinach, and a splash of milk

Days 5-6: Whole-grain cereal with milk and a banana

Day 7: Breakfast burrito with scrambled eggs, cheese, and salsa wrapped in a tortilla

Lunch:

Days 1-2: Turkey and cheese sandwiches with cucumber slices

Days 3-4: Hummus and vegetable wraps with a side of pretzels

Days 5-6: Pasta salad with leftover chicken, veggies, and a light vinaigrette

Day 7: Grilled cheese sandwiches with tomato soup

Dinner:

Days 1-2: Stir-fry with chicken, assorted vegetables, and rice

Days 3-4: Tacos with ground turkey, lettuce, cheese, salsa, and homemade tortillas

Days 5-6: Meatballs made with ground beef, served with spaghetti and marinara sauce

Day 7: Homemade pizza using leftover toppings and a simple dough recipe

Additional Tips for Staying on Track

Budgeting Tools

Use budgeting tools and apps to track your spending and stay on budget. There are many free or low-cost options available that can help you manage your finances and identify areas where you can save more money.

Community Resources

Take advantage of community resources like food banks, farmers' markets, and co-op programs. These can provide affordable or even free food options that can help you stay within your budget.

Cooking Skills

Improving your cooking skills can help you make the most of your groceries and reduce food waste. Learn how to cook with basic ingredients, master a few versatile recipes, and get comfortable with meal prepping and batch cooking.

Family Involvement

Get your family involved in meal planning, shopping, and cooking. This can help them understand the importance of budgeting and encourage them to appreciate the effort that goes into providing healthy meals.

Flexibility and Creativity

Be flexible and creative with your meal plans. Use what you have on hand, experiment with new recipes, and don't be afraid to make substitutions. This can help you adapt to what's available and avoid waste.

The Hidden Agenda of Food Manufacturers

Food manufacturers, in cooperation with Wall Street and advertising agencies, have mastered the art of keeping consumers distracted, overfed, and unhealthy. From addictive additives to cleverly designed packaging, these tactics are all aimed at getting you to buy more, eat more, and ultimately spend more. Understanding this hidden agenda can empower you to make better choices for your family.

A Final Plea: Owing This to Our Families

As parents and caregivers, we owe it to our families to reverse the damage caused by poor financial decisions, overeating, and dependency on convenience foods. It's time to take control of our budgets, our health, and our lives by embracing a more mindful, resourceful approach to eating and spending. By learning to fend for ourselves—whether through cooking from scratch, growing our own food, or simply being more intentional about our choices—we can create a healthier, more sustainable future for our children.

Conclusion

Living on a shoestring budget may seem challenging, but with the right strategies and mindset, it is entirely possible to provide nutritious and satisfying meals for your family without breaking the bank. By focusing on meal planning, smart shopping, reducing waste, and improving your financial literacy, you can transform your family's financial and physical health. Remember, "striving for health is thriving for wealth." The journey may require effort and perseverance, but the rewards of greater knowledge, economical prosperity, and a healthier family are well worth it. Now, let's turn off the distractions, embrace these skills, and start thriving.

Chapter 7

THE COST OF FAST FOOD VS. HOME-COOKED MEALS

Detailed Comparison of Costs

30-Day Grocery List with Estimated Prices

Proteins

- **Whole chickens (2):** $15
- **Ground turkey (6 lbs):** $18
- **Canned tuna (8 cans):** $10
- **Eggs (5 dozen):** $10

- **Peanut butter (2 jars):** $6
- **Dried beans (black beans, lentils, etc.):** $10
- **Chicken breasts (8 lbs):** $20
- **Ground beef (4 lbs):** $16
- **Cheddar cheese (2 lbs):** $8
- **Mozzarella cheese (1 lb):** $4

Grains

- **Brown rice (5 lbs):** $5
- **Whole wheat pasta (6 lbs):** $6
- **Oatmeal (5 lbs):** $5
- **Whole wheat bread (6 loaves):** $12
- **Tortillas (4 packs):** $8
- **Flour (10 lbs):** $5

Dairy

- **Milk (4 gallons):** $12
- **Plain yogurt (2 large tubs):** $6
- **Butter (2 lbs):** $6

Fruits and Vegetables

- **Fresh seasonal vegetables (carrots, potatoes, onions, spinach, bell peppers, broccoli, etc.):** $50
- **Fresh seasonal fruits (apples, bananas, oranges, berries):** $35
- **Canned tomatoes (12 cans):** $12
- **Frozen mixed vegetables (5 bags):** $10
- **Garlic (4 heads):** $2
- **Lemon (4):** $2
- **Avocados (4):** $4

Pantry Staples

- **Olive oil (1 large bottle):** $8
- **Canned tomato sauce (6 cans):** $6
- **Canned beans (6 cans):** $6
- **Sugar (5 lbs):** $4
- **Honey (1 jar):** $4
- **Spices (salt, pepper, garlic powder, cumin, paprika, oregano, etc.):** $10
- **Baking powder, baking soda, yeast:** $4

Miscellaneous

- **Coffee or tea (optional):** $8
- **Cornmeal (for cornbread):** $3

Total Estimated Grocery Cost: $330 - $360

Cost of Eating Out at Various Fast-Food Restaurants for 30 Days

Burger King

- **Average Meal Cost per Person:** $7
- **Family of Four per Day:** $28
- **30 Days:** $28 x 30 = $840

McDonald's

- **Average Meal Cost per Person:** $7
- **Family of Four per Day:** $28
- **30 Days:** $28 x 30 = $840

Rally's (Checkers)

- **Average Meal Cost per Person:** $7
- **Family of Four per Day:** $28
- **30 Days:** $28 x 30 = $840

White Castle

- **Average Meal Cost per Person:** $6
- **Family of Four per Day:** $24
- **30 Days:** $24 x 30 = $720

Jimmy John's

- **Average Meal Cost per Person:** $8
- **Family of Four per Day:** $32
- **30 Days:** $32 x 30 = $960

Average Monthly Fast Food Cost for One Meal Per Day: $600 - $960

Summary of Cost Comparison:

- **Total Monthly Grocery Cost:** $330 - $360
- **Average Monthly Fast Food Cost for One Meal Per Day:** $600 - $960

Savings from Home-Cooked Meals:

- **Low Estimate:** $600 (fast food) - $360 (grocery) = $240 saved
- **High Estimate:** $960 (fast food) - $330 (grocery) = $630 saved

Health Benefits of Home-Cooked Meals vs. Fast Food

Health Benefits of Eating Home-Cooked Meals Using the Ingredients in This Book:

Nutrient-Dense Meals:

Balanced Nutrition: Home-cooked meals using whole ingredients like fresh vegetables, lean proteins, and whole grains ensure that your family gets a balanced diet rich in essential nutrients, including vitamins, minerals, and fiber.

Portion Control: Preparing meals at home allows you to control portion sizes, reducing the risk of overeating and promoting a healthy weight.

Less Processed Food: Home-cooked meals avoid the excessive use of preservatives, additives, and artificial ingredients commonly found in processed foods, which can contribute to various health issues.

Reduced Sodium and Sugar Intake:

Lower Sodium: Fast food meals are often high in sodium, which can lead to high blood pressure and increase the risk of heart disease. Home-cooked meals allow you to control the amount of salt used, promoting better heart health.

Reduced Sugar: Fast food often contains added sugars in unexpected places, such as sauces and bread. By cooking at home, you can minimize the use of added sugars, helping to prevent weight gain and lower the risk of developing diabetes.

Better Fat Quality:

Healthy Fats: Home cooking allows you to choose healthier fats, such as olive oil, over the trans fats and unhealthy oils often used in fast food. This helps lower bad cholesterol levels and supports overall cardiovascular health.

Less Saturated Fat: Fast food items are often high in saturated fat, which can raise cholesterol levels and increase the risk of heart disease. Home-cooked meals using lean meats and low-fat dairy help reduce these risks.

Increased Fiber Intake:

Whole Grains and Vegetables: The meal plans in this book emphasize whole grains like brown rice and whole wheat pasta, as well as fiber-rich vegetables, which support digestive health and help maintain healthy cholesterol levels.

Positive Impact on Mental Health:

Cooking as a Family Activity: Preparing and eating meals together as a family fosters connection, reduces stress, and can improve mental well-being. Sharing a meal at home can also create a routine and provide stability, which is beneficial for mental health.

Health Ramifications of Regularly Eating Fast Food:

High Caloric Intake and Weight Gain:

Calorie-Dense Meals: Fast food meals are typically high in calories, often exceeding the daily caloric needs in just one meal. Regular consumption can lead to weight gain and obesity, which are risk factors for many chronic diseases.

Lack of Nutritional Balance: Fast food meals often lack the balance of macronutrients (carbohydrates, fats, and proteins) and are deficient in essential vitamins and minerals, leading to potential nutrient deficiencies.

Increased Risk of Heart Disease:

High Saturated Fat and Trans Fats: Fast food is often high in unhealthy fats that contribute to the buildup of plaque in the arteries, increasing the risk of heart disease and stroke.

Excessive Sodium: The high sodium content in fast food contributes to elevated blood pressure and is a major risk factor for cardiovascular diseases.

Higher Risk of Diabetes:

Added Sugars: Fast food often contains large amounts of added sugars, which can spike blood sugar levels and increase the risk of insulin resistance and type 2 diabetes.

Low Fiber: The lack of fiber in fast food diets contributes to poor blood sugar control and can exacerbate the risk of developing diabetes.

Digestive Issues:

Low Fiber Intake: The typical fast food diet lacks fiber, which can lead to digestive issues such as constipation and an increased risk of developing gastrointestinal disorders.

High in Additives: Fast food often contains preservatives and additives that can irritate the digestive system and lead to long-term health issues.

Negative Impact on Mental Health:

Increased Stress and Anxiety: The lack of routine and connection in fast food consumption, combined with the poor nutritional profile of these foods, can negatively affect mental health, contributing to stress, anxiety, and depression.

RESTAURE OUT
EATING OUT

HEALTH BEADY
HOME-COOKED MEALS
HEALTH
RUPPORTE
MEALTH FEAD
WEALD GREAHS
HEIDAL FEALTH
ROSITIVE
HEALTH
HEALTH
FEAD
FOOD

APPENDIX

30-Day Grocery List with Estimated Prices

Proteins

- **Whole chickens (2):** $15
- **Ground turkey (6 lbs):** $18
- **Canned tuna (8 cans):** $10
- **Eggs (5 dozen):** $10
- **Peanut butter (2 jars):** $6
- **Dried beans (black beans, lentils, etc.):** $10
- **Chicken breasts (8 lbs):** $20
- **Ground beef (4 lbs):** $16
- **Cheddar cheese (2 lbs):** $8
- **Mozzarella cheese (1 lb):** $4

Grains

- **Brown rice (5 lbs):** $5
- **Whole wheat pasta (6 lbs):** $6
- **Oatmeal (5 lbs):** $5
- **Whole wheat bread (6 loaves):** $12

- **Tortillas (4 packs):** $8
- **Flour (10 lbs):** $5

Dairy

- **Milk (4 gallons):** $12
- **Plain yogurt (2 large tubs):** $6
- **Butter (2 lbs):** $6

Fruits and Vegetables

- **Fresh seasonal vegetables (carrots, potatoes, onions, spinach, bell peppers, broccoli, etc.):** $50
- **Fresh seasonal fruits (apples, bananas, oranges, berries):** $35
- **Canned tomatoes (12 cans):** $12
- **Frozen mixed vegetables (5 bags):** $10
- **Garlic (4 heads):** $2
- **Lemon (4):** $2
- **Avocados (4):** $4

Pantry Staples

- **Olive oil (1 large bottle):** $8
- **Canned tomato sauce (6 cans):** $6
- **Canned beans (6 cans):** $6

- **Sugar (5 lbs):** $4
- **Honey (1 jar):** $4
- **Spices (salt, pepper, garlic powder, cumin, paprika, oregano, etc.):** $10
- **Baking powder, baking soda, yeast:** $4

Miscellaneous

- **Coffee or tea (optional):** $8
- **Cornmeal (for cornbread):** $3
- **Total Estimated Grocery Cost:** $330 - $360

Sample Weekly Meal Plans

Week 1:

Day 1:

- **Breakfast:** Oatmeal with cinnamon and apple slices.
- **Lunch:** Peanut butter and jelly sandwiches with carrot sticks.
- **Dinner:** Roasted chicken with roasted potatoes and steamed broccoli.
- **Leftover Plan:** Save leftover chicken for chicken salad and soup.

Day 2:

- **Breakfast:** Scrambled eggs with toast.
- **Lunch:** Chicken salad wraps with spinach and a side of fruit.
- **Dinner:** Spaghetti with homemade tomato sauce and a side salad.
- **Leftover Plan:** Use leftover pasta for a cold pasta salad later in the week.

Day 3:

- **Breakfast:** Yogurt with honey and granola.
- **Lunch:** Leftover spaghetti with a side of steamed vegetables.
- **Dinner:** Black bean and cheese quesadillas with a side of rice.
- **Leftover Plan:** Save leftover rice for stir-fry.

Day 4:

- **Breakfast:** Smoothie with frozen fruit, spinach, and milk.
- **Lunch:** Black bean soup with whole wheat bread.
- **Dinner:** Stir-fried vegetables with rice and scrambled eggs.
- **Leftover Plan:** Save some stir-fried vegetables for a stir-fry omelet.

Day 5:

- **Breakfast:** Pancakes with fresh fruit.
- **Lunch:** Tuna salad sandwiches with a side of cucumber slices.
- **Dinner:** Chicken and vegetable stir-fry with rice.
- **Leftover Plan:** Save some stir-fried chicken and vegetables for wraps.

Day 6:

- **Breakfast:** Yogurt with honey and granola.
- **Lunch:** Chicken and vegetable wraps with a side of fruit.
- **Dinner:** Lentil soup with whole wheat bread.
- **Leftover Plan:** Use leftover soup for a quick lunch the next day.

Day 7:

- **Breakfast:** Scrambled eggs with toast and fruit.
- **Lunch:** Leftover lentil soup with a side salad.
- **Dinner:** Homemade pizza with leftover vegetables and cheese.
- **Leftover Plan:** Save some pizza for lunch the next day.

Week 2:

Day 8:

- **Breakfast:** Oatmeal with banana slices.
- **Lunch:** Leftover pizza slices with a side of fruit.
- **Dinner:** Ground turkey tacos with lettuce, cheese, and homemade salsa.
- **Leftover Plan:** Save leftover taco filling for taco bowls.

Day 9:

- **Breakfast:** Smoothie with frozen fruit, spinach, and milk.
- **Lunch:** Taco bowls with rice, beans, and leftover taco filling.
- **Dinner:** Baked chicken with sweet potatoes and green beans.
- **Leftover Plan:** Use leftover chicken for chicken and rice casserole.

Day 10:

- **Breakfast:** Yogurt with honey and granola.
- **Lunch:** Chicken and rice casserole with a side salad.
- **Dinner:** Spaghetti with ground turkey and tomato sauce.
- **Leftover Plan:** Use leftover spaghetti for spaghetti pie.

Day 11:

- **Breakfast:** Scrambled eggs with toast and fruit.
- **Lunch:** Spaghetti pie with a side of steamed vegetables.
- **Dinner:** Vegetable stir-fry with rice and tofu (or leftover chicken).
- **Leftover Plan:** Save some stir-fried vegetables for a stir-fry omelet.

Day 12:

- **Breakfast:** Pancakes with fresh fruit.
- **Lunch:** Tuna salad sandwiches with a side of cucumber slices.
- **Dinner:** Ground turkey and bean chili with cornbread.
- **Leftover Plan:** Save leftover chili for chili baked potatoes.

Day 13:

- **Breakfast:** Oatmeal with cinnamon and apple slices.
- **Lunch:** Chili baked potatoes with cheese and a side of steamed broccoli.
- **Dinner:** Homemade vegetable soup with whole wheat bread.
- **Leftover Plan:** Save leftover soup for lunch the next day.

Day 14:

- **Breakfast:** Yogurt with honey and granola.
- **Lunch:** Leftover vegetable soup with a side salad.
- **Dinner:** Baked ziti with ground turkey, tomato sauce, and cheese.
- **Leftover Plan:** Save leftover ziti for lunch the next day.

Week 3:

Day 15:

- **Breakfast:** Smoothie with frozen fruit, spinach, and milk.
- **Lunch:** Leftover baked ziti with a side of steamed vegetables.
- **Dinner:** Chicken and vegetable stir-fry with rice.
- **Leftover Plan:** Save some stir-fried chicken and vegetables for wraps.

Day 16:

- **Breakfast:** Oatmeal with banana slices.
- **Lunch:** Chicken and vegetable wraps with a side of fruit.
- **Dinner:** Black bean and cheese quesadillas with a side of rice.
- **Leftover Plan:** Save leftover rice for fried rice.

Day 17:

- **Breakfast:** Scrambled eggs with toast and fruit.
- **Lunch:** Leftover quesadillas with a side salad.
- **Dinner:** Fried rice with scrambled eggs, vegetables, and leftover chicken.

- **Leftover Plan:** Save leftover fried rice for a quick lunch the next day.

Day 18:

- **Breakfast:** Yogurt with honey and granola.
- **Lunch:** Leftover fried rice with a side of fruit.
- **Dinner:** Lentil stew with whole wheat bread.
- **Leftover Plan:** Save leftover stew for lunch the next day.

Day 19:

- **Breakfast:** Pancakes with fresh fruit.
- **Lunch:** Leftover lentil stew with a side salad.
- **Dinner:** Turkey meatballs with spaghetti and marinara sauce.
- **Leftover Plan:** Save leftover meatballs for meatball subs.

Day 20:

- **Breakfast:** Smoothie with frozen fruit, spinach, and milk.
- **Lunch:** Meatball subs with a side of carrot sticks.
- **Dinner:** Roasted chicken with mashed potatoes and green beans.
- **Leftover Plan:** Save leftover chicken for chicken salad and soup.

Day 21:

- **Breakfast:** Oatmeal with cinnamon and apple slices.
- **Lunch:** Chicken salad sandwiches with a side of fruit.
- **Dinner:** Vegetable and chicken stir-fry with rice.
- **Leftover Plan:** Save some stir-fried chicken and vegetables for stir-fry omelet.

Week 4:

Day 22:

- **Breakfast:** Scrambled eggs with toast and fruit.
- **Lunch:** Stir-fry omelet with a side of whole wheat toast.
- **Dinner:** Black bean soup with whole wheat bread.
- **Leftover Plan:** Use leftover soup for a quick lunch the next day.

Day 23:

- **Breakfast:** Yogurt with honey and granola.
- **Lunch:** Leftover black bean soup with a side salad.
- **Dinner:** Baked ziti with ground turkey, tomato sauce, and cheese.
- **Leftover Plan:** Save leftover ziti for lunch the next day.

ABOUT THE AUTHORS

Corwin Watson is a former Navy Corpsman turned entrepreneur, film producer, and author. His passion for financial literacy and helping others thrive on a budget has led him to share his strategies and insights in this book. Corwin is dedicated to empowering families to take control of their finances and live healthier, more fulfilling lives.

Janine Madison is an expert product reviewer and entrepreneur known for her attention to detail and commitment to quality. She brings her experience and insights into smart shopping, budgeting, and healthy living to this guide, helping families make informed decisions that benefit their financial and physical well-being.

PUBLISHING INFORMATION

Thriving on a Shoestring Budget: A Guide to Nourishing Your Family on $300 to $400 a Month

Published by RebuildUS Publishing

SIGN UP FOR MY AUTHOR NEWSLETTER

Be the first to learn about Corwin Watson's new releases and receive exclusive content for readers and writers!

www.rebuildnus.com

ABOUT THE AUTHOR

Corwin Watson** is an entrepreneur, inventor, filmmaker, and author with a passion for empowering families to thrive in challenging circumstances. Drawing from a wealth of personal experience and professional knowledge, Corwin has spent years helping individuals and families navigate financial hardships, mental health challenges, and personal growth. His innovative approaches and practical solutions have impacted countless lives, guiding them toward a path of resilience, self-sufficiency, and hope.

As the founder of *Rebuild US, LLC*, Corwin has dedicated his career to creating resources and opportunities that foster strong communities and healthy relationships. His multifaceted company provides services ranging from video production and property development to consulting and mobile app development. Corwin's work is deeply rooted in his commitment to making a difference, especially in the lives of those who face adversity.

In *Thriving on a Shoestring Budget: A Guide to Nourishing Your Family on $300 to $400 a Month*, Corwin combines his expertise in financial literacy with his personal insights on family dynamics, offering readers a practical guide to living well on a limited budget. This book is not just a manual for cutting costs; it's a blueprint for building a better life, one meal and one choice at a time.

Corwin is also the author of several other works, including *Road to Nowhere: How I'm Saving Myself from the Self-Destructive Behavior that Ruled Me* and *Don't Even Think About Getting Married - Until the Costs are Weighed.* Through his writing, Corwin continues to inspire and uplift, encouraging readers to overcome obstacles and thrive in every aspect of their lives.

When he's not writing or working on his next big project, Corwin enjoys spending time with his family, exploring new ideas, and pursuing his mission to create lasting, positive change in the world.

ACKNOWLEDGMENTS

First and foremost, I want to thank God for giving me the strength and wisdom to write this book. Without His guidance, none of this would be possible.

To my children—Corwin Jr., Erin, Ariel, Cambridge, Carraghan, and Charlotte—you are my greatest inspiration. Your smiles and laughter remind me daily why I do this work. I hope this book will serve as a foundation for the values and resilience I strive to instill in you.

I want to extend my deepest gratitude to everyone at *Rebuild US, LLC*, for believing in my vision and helping me turn it into reality. Your dedication and hard work are the driving forces behind our success. To my mentors and colleagues, thank you for your invaluable advice and guidance.

A special thanks to Janine Madison for her insightful feedback and honest critiques during the development of this book. Your attention to detail and unique perspective have made this project stronger.

To all the families and individuals who have shared their stories with me over the years—this book is for you. Your resilience and determination have shown me what it truly means to thrive, no matter the circumstances.

Lastly, I want to thank my readers. This book serves as a beacon of hope and a practical guide to living well, even on the tightest of budgets. Your journey toward financial freedom and family nourishment is important, and I'm honored to be a part of it.

Thank you all.

Corwin Watson

Made in the USA
Monee, IL
03 November 2026

67379478R00059